A Poet's Heart

Rev. Dr. Gregory C. Wright

A Poet's Heart

Copyright ©1997 by Gregory Cecil Wright/ Fire Heart, Inc.

All rights reserved. No part of this book may be reproduced or transmitted in any form or by any means, electronic or mechanical, including photocopying, recording, or by any information storage and retrieval system, without permission in writing from the copyright owner.

All Scriptural references come from the New International Version.

Table of Contents

Anticipation……………………………………………….1

As I Journey………………………………………….…...3

Beauty…………………………………………………….5

Because You Know Me…………………………………..7

Believe In Me…………………………………………….9

Come……………………………………………………11

Delighted In You………………………………………..13

Faith…………………………………………………….15

Free……………………………………………………..17

In The Serenity of Praises………………………………19

Life……………………………………………………...21

Moments Like These……………………………….…...23

My Deepest Thanks……………………………………..25

My Desire……………………………………………….27

My Word………………………………………………..29

Please Come Back………………………………………31

Recognizing Change……………………………………33

Son Rises………………………………………………..35

The Call…………………………………………………37

The Goal………………………………………………...39

About the Author/From the Author……………………..41

"Anticipation"

Whether we realize it or not, we are in a war (even a spiritual one) over our souls and over our eternal destination. We must be strong and daily put on the whole armor of God.

Ephesians 6:10-18

"Finally, be strong in the Lord and in his mighty power. Put on the full armor of God, so that you can take your stand against the devil's schemes. For our struggle is not against flesh and blood, but against the rulers, against the authorities, against the powers of this dark world and against the spiritual forces of evil in the heavenly realms. Therefore, put on the full armor of God, so that when the day of evil comes, you may be able to stand your ground, and after you have done everything, to stand. Stand firm then, with the belt of truth buckled around your waist, with the breastplate of righteousness in place, and with your feet fitted with the readiness that comes from the gospel of peace. In addition to all this, take up the shield of faith, with which you can extinguish all the flaming arrows of the evil one. Take the helmet of salvation and the sword of the Spirit, which is the word of God. And pray in the Spirit on all occasions with all kinds of prayers and requests. With this in mind, be alert and always keep on praying for all the Lord's people." (New International Version)

THIS IS A PROMISE FROM GOD: ISAIAH 51:5

"My righteousness draws near speedily, my salvation is on the way, and my arm will bring justice to the nations. The islands will look to me and wait in hope for my arm."

Hearts are burning. Lights are flickering.

There is a war in the heavenlies, and all
Stand in the "narrow way."

Hearts are pounding. Lights are soaring.

There is a fierce battle taking place, and

All await, pray, and praise God – for

The victory belongs to the Lord.

He, and only He, reigns triumphant.

"As I Journey"

Psalm 9:9-10

"The LORD is a refuge for the oppressed, a stronghold in times of trouble. Those who know your name will trust in you, for you, LORD, have never forsaken those who seek you."

Proverbs 18:10

"The name of the Lord is a fortified tower; the righteous run to it and are safe."

Jeremiah 33:3

"Call to me and I will answer you and tell you great and unsearchable things you do not know."

THIS IS A PROMISE FROM OUR LORD TO THE CHURCH AT PHILADELPHIA IN REVELATION 3:7 -8.

"To the angel of the church in Philadelphia write: These are the words of him who is holy and true, who holds the key of David. What he opens no one can shut, and what he shuts no one can open, I know your deeds. See, I have placed before you an open door that no one can shut. I know that you have little strength, yet you have kept my word and have not denied my name."

As I journey through the course of time,
I will always remember the Lord Divine.
Though heartbreaks come, and the winds
May blow, I will always call on the name
I know. God is His name, and He is always
The same. In grief and despair, He is my
Relief. His words of comfort soothe me. In
My trials, He is always there to cheer me up
And make me aware that nobody can
Challenge His love for me because His love
Is strong and lasts for eternity.

"Beauty"

I Samuel 16:7

But the Lord said to Samuel, "Do not consider his appearance or his height, for I have rejected him. The Lord does not look at the things people look at. People look at the outward appearance, but the Lord looks at the heart."

Matthew 5:8

"Blessed are the pure in heart, for they will see God."

Matthew 12:34-35

"You brood of vipers, how can you who are evil say anything good? For the mouth speaks what the heart is full of. A good man brings good things out of the good stored up in him, and an evil man brings evil things out of the evil stored up in him."

**THIS IS A RESULT OF HAVING A PURE HEART BEFORE GOD:
Psalm 24:4-5**

"The one who has clean hands and a pure heart, who does not trust in an idol or swear by a false god. They will receive blessing from the Lord and vindication from God their Savior."

Many define beauty as the outward appearance,
While some define it as the character of a person.
However, I define beauty as radiance. It comes
From what the person has on the inside. Beauty
Is not skin deep but "heart" deep. It is the heart
From whence cometh the essence of beauty. I see
Beauty as undefiled truth and honesty.

"Because You Know Me"

Matthew 12:47-50

"Someone told him, "Your mother and brothers are standing outside, wanting to speak to you." He replied to him, "Who is my mother, and who are my brothers?" Pointing to his disciples, he said, "Here are my mother and my brothers. For whoever does the will of my Father in heaven is my brother and sister and mother.""

John 15:9-10

"As the Father has loved me, so have I loved you. Now remain in my love. If you keep my commands, you will remain in my love, just as I have kept my Father's commands and remain in his love."

Romans 5:8

"But God demonstrates his own love for us in this: While we were still sinners, Christ died for us."

Because you know Me, I can say,
"Do My Will with all of your being."
Because you know Me, I can say,
"The race is not given to the swift nor to
The strong but to the one who
Endures till the end."
Because you know Me, I can say,
"Take eat. This is My body which is
Given for you: this do in remembrance
Of me."
Because you know Me, I can say,
"You are loved in every way there is to be loved."

"Believe In Me"

II Chronicles 20:20

"Early in the morning they left for the Desert of Tekoa. As they set out, Jehoshaphat stood and said, "Listen to me, Judah and people of Jerusalem! Have faith in the LORD your God and you will be upheld; have faith in his prophets and you will be successful.""

John 1:12-13

"Yet to all who did receive him, to those who believed in his name, he gave the right to become children of God— children born not of natural descent, nor of human decision or a husband's will, but born of God."

I Thessalonians 5:23-24

"May God himself, the God of peace, sanctify you through and through. May your whole spirit, soul and body be kept blameless at the coming of our Lord Jesus Christ. The one who calls you is faithful, and he will do it."

Something to Ponder:

Our faith in God and our belief in His Son, Jesus Christ, will be our life support in the upcoming years. God is calling us to believe in Him, and our actions speak louder than words.

Believe in Me as I have given you a world
You thought was impossible for you. Believe
In Me being that I have delivered you from a
Lifestyle of shame and have clothed you with
My righteousness. Believe in Me because
Without Me you would be dead. Believe in Me
For I Am the One who has the best in store for you.
Believe in Me.

"Come"

Matthew 11:28-30

"Come to me, all you who labor and are heavy laden, and I will give you rest. Take my yoke upon you and learn from me, for I am gentle and humble in heart, and you will find rest for your souls. For my yoke is easy, and my burden is light."

Psalm 95:7-9

"Today, if only you would hear his voice, "Do not harden your hearts as you did at Meribah, as you did that day at Massah in the wilderness, where your ancestors tested me; they tried me, though they had seen what I did."

Matthew 7:13-14

"Enter through the narrow gate. For wide is the gate and broad is the road that leads to destruction, and many enter through it. But small is the gate and narrow the road that leads to life, and only a few find it."

THIS IS WHAT OUR LORD AND SAVIOR JESUS CHRIST HAS SAID AND IS STILL SAYING, EVEN TODAY.

Revelation 3:19-22

"Those whom I love I rebuke and discipline. So be earnest and repent. Here I am! I stand at the door and knock. If anyone hears my voice and opens the door, I will come in and eat with that person, and they with me. To the one who is victorious, I will give the right to sit with me on my throne, just as I was victorious and sat down with my Father on his throne. Whoever has ears, let them hear what the Spirit says to the churches."

Come one. Come all into the House. Put off the
Cares of your everyday lives and enter in through
The front door.
Come one. Come all into the House. Run no
More, but stop, listen, hear Me, and obey Me.
Come one. Come all into the house. A terrible
Storm is about to come and destroy all those who
Are caught without a covering.
Come one. Come all. This is the day of your
Salvation.
Come.

"Delighted In You"

Psalm 37:4-5

"Take delight in the Lord, and he will give you the desires of your heart. Commit your way to the LORD; trust in him, and he will do this."

Sometimes, no matter what we do or say, we do not believe God really loves us or even that we can do enough to please Him. However, God desires for us to seek Him and to believe Him and His Word He has set before us. We must believe that God truly loves us and that He will forgive us of our sins if we repent. John 3:16-17 says, "For God so loved the world that he gave his one and only Son, that whoever believes in him shall not perish but have everlasting life. For God did not send his Son into the world to condemn the world but to save world through him." Also, in Romans 8:1, Paul wrote, "Therefore, there is now no condemnation for those who are in Christ Jesus." So, be encouraged and remember that no matter what situation you are facing God loves you and so does our Lord and Savior Jesus Christ. Remember this:

"But God demonstrates his own love for us in this: While we were still sinners, Christ died for us." (Romans 5:8)

Why are you so down? I'm delighted in **You.**

Why are you so depressed? **I Am** delighted in you.

Why do you worry? I'm delighted in **You.**

Why do you doubt My love? **I Am** delighted in you!!!

"Faith"

Hebrews 11:1-3

"Now faith is confidence in what we hope for and assurance about what we do not see. This is what the ancients were commended for. By faith we understand that the universe was formed at God's command, so that what is seen was not made out of what was visible."

Hebrews 12:1-2

"Therefore, since we are surrounded by such a great cloud of witnesses, let us throw off everything that hinders and the sin that so easily entangles. And let us run with perseverance the race marked out for us, fixing our eyes on Jesus, the pioneer and perfecter of faith. For the joy set before him he endured the cross, scorning its shame, and sat down at the right hand of the throne of God."

Revelation 12:10-11

"Then I heard a loud voice in heaven say:

"Now have come the salvation and the power
   and the kingdom of our God,
   and the authority of his Messiah.
For the accuser of our brothers and sisters,
   who accuses them before our God day and night,
   has been hurled down.
They triumphed over him
   by the blood of the Lamb
   and by the word of their testimony;
they did not love their lives so much
   as to shrink from death.""

Our faith speaks louder than our words and produces action. God will judge us by what we have said and by what we have done.

Faith believes – does not doubt.

Faith learns – does not stop.

Faith leaps – does not stay down.

Faith encourages – does not complain.

Faith loves – does not hate.

Faith keeps on going – does not hesitate.

Faith is consistent – does not waiver.

And faith forgives – does not destroy.

"Free"

What does it mean to be free? To be free is to no longer be chained by events in our past. When God draws us to him by His Holy Spirit and we accept Jesus Christ as Lord of our lives, our past sins are washed away by the blood of Jesus, and God no longer sees our sins. We now have the chance to walk **free** of our past bondage(s) and walk and live in the power of the Holy Spirit.

HOWEVER, IT IS OUR DECISION TO BE FREE. WE MUST DESIRE TO BE FREE AND FOR GOD TO FREE US. ONCE WE HAVE PRAYED FOR THIS TO HAPPEN, WE MUST BELIEVE WHAT GOD'S WORD SAYS AND MUST BELIEVE THAT GOD WILL ANSWER OUR PRAYERS.

Romans 8:1-5

"Therefore, there is now no condemnation for those who are in Christ Jesus, because through Christ Jesus the law of the Spirit who gives life has set you free from the law of sin and death. For what the law was powerless to do because it was weakened by the flesh, God did by sending his own Son in the likeness of sinful flesh to be a sin offering. And so he condemned sin in the flesh, in order that the righteous requirement of the law might be fully met in us, who do not live according to the flesh but according to the Spirit. Those who live according to the flesh have their minds set on what the flesh desires; but those who live in accordance with the Spirit have their minds set on what the Spirit desires."

And with the "freedom" we have through Christ, we must remember to keep our eyes on Jesus and spread the Gospel wherever we go and keep going forward in the Name of our Lord and Savior Jesus Christ.

Romans 5:1

"Therefore, since we have been justified through faith, we have peace with God through our Lord Jesus Christ."

The prisoner's gates open. The latch is pulled up
And high above the locks. The light is green, and
All is well. The prisoner is told he is free and that
He may proceed through the gates. As the
Prisoner walks through these tall, dark gates, he is
Told never to return, not even to turn around to
Look upon the "gloom" of his past. He is told
Again that he is free and that Freedom's made
Him free. Then suddenly, the man raises his arms
And exclaims with a shout, "I'm free!!!"

"In The Serenity of Praises"

Psalm 28:7

"The Lord is my strength and my shield; my heart trusts in him, and he helps me. My heart leaps for joy, and with my song I praise Him."

Psalm 92:1-2

"It is good to praise the Lord and make music to your name, O Most High, proclaiming your love in the morning
and your faithfulness at night."

Psalm 118:24

"The Lord has done it this very day; let us rejoice today and be glad."

A reminder: God loves His people to praise Him. As we do, His Holy Spirit comes and rests and dwells in the midst of His people.

Praises are heard all around.

The sounds echo across the mountain paths.

These sounds, full of glory and grace, extend

Upward towards the heavens.

Gently and quietly, the water rifts down the

Waterfall as the Spirit of the Living God dwells

And rests on the praises of His people.

"Life"

Matthew 7:7 -8

"Ask and it will be given to you; seek and you will find; knock and the door will be opened to you. For everyone who asks receives; the one who seeks finds; and to the one who knocks, the door will be opened."

Matthew 12:7

"If you had known what these words mean, 'I desire mercy, not sacrifice,' you would not have condemned the innocent."

Romans 8:13

"For if you live according to the flesh, you will die; but if by the Spirit you put to death the misdeeds of the body, you will live."

The choices we make in our lives will determine our future. We must be wise and prayerful about the choices we make. Our choices can result in life or death. Choose wisely!

Life is a choice, so choose.

Life is an adventure, but

You must dare to go forward.

Life is a challenge, so try it.

Life is a mystery, but

You must decide to seek

Truth.

"Moments Like These"

Jeremiah 32:37-41

"I will surely gather them from all the lands where I banish them in my furious anger and great wrath; I will bring them back to this place and let them live in safety. They will be my people, and I will be their God. I will give them singleness of heart and action, so that they will always fear me and that all will then go well for them and for their children after them. I will make an everlasting covenant with them: I will never stop doing good to them, and I will inspire them to fear me, so that they will never turn away from me. I will rejoice in doing them good and will assuredly plant them in this land with all my heart and soul."

Moments like these make history in my
Heart. Just the thought of them bring back
Memories of happiness.
Moments like these help me to stand, understand
Life better, and be ready for what is to come.
Moments like these fill me with so much
Peace and joy, that I wish I could fly and soar in
This joy forever.

"My Deepest Thanks To You"

Isaiah 55:6-7

"Seek the LORD while he may be found; call on him while he is near. Let the wicked forsake their ways and the unrighteous their thoughts Let them turn to the LORD, and he will have mercy on them, and to our God, for he will freely pardon."

Matthew 7:21-23

"Not everyone who says to me, 'Lord, Lord,' will enter the kingdom of heaven, but only the one who does the will of my Father who is in heaven. Many will say to me on that day, 'Lord, Lord, did we not prophesy in your name and in your name drive out demons and in your name perform many miracles?' Then I will tell them plainly, 'I never knew you. Away from me, you evildoers!'"

Luke 21:34-36

"Be careful, or your hearts will be weighed down with carousing, drunkenness and the anxieties of life, and that day will close on you suddenly like a trap. For it will come on all those who live on the face of the whole earth. Be always on the watch, and pray that you may be able to escape all that is about to happen, and that you may be able to stand before the Son of Man."

We are living in perilous times, and it is time for us to return to the Lord with our whole hearts. We do not know the time or the day when the Lord will return. So, repent and today start anew. If you have not accepted Jesus Christ into your heart, you can do so right now. Just ask Him to come into your heart this very moment. Your sins will be forgiven, and you will have a new life that is awaiting you. The opportunity for salvation is right now. In Revelation 3:19-21, Jesus the Son of the Living God, said the following things:

"Those whom I love I rebuke and discipline. So be earnest and repent. Here I am! I stand at the door and knock. If anyone hears my voice and opens the door, I will come in and eat with that person, and they with me. To the one who is victorious, I will give the right to sit with me on my throne, just as I was victorious and sat down with my Father on his throne."

Many times, I pass by You and don't call Your Name. Sometimes, I take You for granted and Do not even stop to talk. Many times, I see You At work in my life and smile or even grin. Sometimes, I even say "Hello" and ask for Your Help. Well, God, I am sorry and repent for my Mistakes. After this long time, I have come to Realize that I need You to be the love of my life. So, my deepest regrets do I plead to You right Now. Please forgive me Lord, my God.
Here are my deepest thanks to You.

"My Desire"

Psalm 25:12-13

"Who, then, are those who fear the LORD? He will instruct them in the ways they should choose. They will spend their days in prosperity, and their descendants will inherit the land."

Jeremiah 33:3

"Call to me and I will answer you and tell you great and unsearchable things you do not know."

Matthew 6:33

"But seek first his kingdom and his righteousness, and all these things will be given to you as well."

If our desire is to know God's Will for our lives, we must forsake our idols and seek God, and God will come and dwell within us. The following was recorded in II Corinthians 6:16-18:

"What agreement is there between the temple of God and idols? For we are the temple of the living God. As God has said: "I will live with them and walk among them, and I will be their God, and they will be my people." Therefore, "Come out from them and be separate, says the Lord. Touch no unclean thing, and I will receive you." And, "I will be a Father to you,
and you will be my sons and daughters, says the Lord Almighty."

My desire is to see those things I have never seen Before. My desire is to see those things only You Can show me, for I do know that You will answer Me and show me great and mighty things. Your Word says so, and I believe it. My desire is to Know and to see Your desire- Your heart for Your People.

"My Word"

Isaiah 44:21-23

""Remember these things, Jacob, for you, Israel, are my servant. I have made you, you are my servant; Israel, I will not forget you. I have swept away your offenses like a cloud, your sins like the morning mist. Return to me, for I have redeemed you." Sing for joy, you heavens, for the LORD has done this; shout aloud, you earth beneath. Burst into song, you mountains, you forests and all your trees, for the LORD has redeemed Jacob, he displays his glory in Israel."

Luke 4:18-19

"The Spirit of the Lord is on me, because he has anointed me
 to proclaim good news to the poor. He has sent me to proclaim freedom for the prisoners and recovery of sight for the blind,
to set the oppressed free, to proclaim the year of the Lord's favor."

Hebrews 4:12

"For the word of God is alive and active. Sharper than any double-edged sword, it penetrates even to dividing soul and spirit, joints and marrow; it judges the thoughts and attitudes of the heart."

My **Word** can kill sin and take it far away.

My **Word** can heal the broken-hearted and give

Them a Second chance again.

My **Word** can give life to those who are dead.

My **Word** can free the bound and loose them to

Their destiny.

"Please Come Back"

Matthew 12:31-32

"And so I tell you, every kind of sin and slander can be forgiven, but blasphemy against the Spirit will not be forgiven. Anyone who speaks a word against the Son of Man will be forgiven, but anyone who speaks against the Holy Spirit will not be forgiven, either in this age or in the age to come."

John 14:26

"But the Advocate, the Holy Spirit, whom the Father will send in my name, will teach you all things and will remind you of everything I have said to you."

Galatians 5:16-26

"So I say, walk by the Spirit, and you will not gratify the desires of the flesh. For the flesh desires what is contrary to the Spirit and the Spirit what is contrary to the flesh. They are in conflict with each other, so that you are not to do whatever you want. But if you are led by the Spirit, you are not under the law. The acts of the flesh are obvious: sexual immorality, impurity and debauchery; idolatry and witchcraft; hatred, discord, jealousy, fits of rage, selfish ambition, dissensions, factions and envy; drunkenness, orgies, and the like. I warn you, as I did before, that those who live like this will not inherit the kingdom of God. But the fruit of the Spirit is love, joy, peace, forbearance, kindness, goodness, faithfulness, gentleness and self-control. Against such things, there is no law. Those who belong to Christ Jesus have crucified the flesh with its passions and desires. Since we live by the Spirit, let us keep in step with the Spirit. Let us not become conceited, provoking and envying each other."

Holy Spirit, please come back.

I apologize for the things that I have done.

Holy Spirit, please come back.

I have realized that I need You in order to grow.

Holy Spirit, please come back.

I would never be the same without You.

Holy Spirit, please come back.

You have changed my life and have given me hope.

"Recognizing Change"

Proverbs 3: 5-6

"Trust in the LORD with all your heart and lean not on your own understanding; in all your ways submit to him, and he will make your paths straight."

Ecclesiastes 3:1-8

There is a time for everything,

and a season for every activity under the heavens:

a time to be born and a time to die,
a time to plant and a time to uproot,
a time to kill and a time to heal,

a time to tear down and a time to build,
a time to weep and a time to laugh,
a time to mourn and a time to dance,
a time to scatter stones and a time to gather them,
a time to embrace and a time to refrain from embracing,

a time to search and a time to give up,
a time to keep and a time to throw away,
a time to tear and a time to mend,
a time to be silent and a time to speak,
a time to love and a time to hate,
a time for war and a time for peace.

Change is something that we, as human beings, sometimes try to avoid but cannot. Sometimes, we are faced with decisions we do not want to make. Other times, we just do not want to have to "start all over" again. Whatever you are dealing with in your own life, remember that change is not always bad. Your blessing might come from that particular change, even though you do not see it. But, be encouraged and know that the Lord thy God is with you in this change and that He will not leave you nor forsake you.

Recognizing change brings forth a reaction – whether good or bad.

When change comes, some of us run from it, so we will not have to deal with it. But no matter how much you run from it, you will have to deal with it. Change is not always bad. Neither is disappointment.

You are going to have disappointments in this life.

It is the way that you deal with them.

Change is inevitable.

You just grow into

it.

"Son Rises"

John 15:8-17

"This is to my Father's glory, that you bear much fruit, showing yourselves to be my disciples. As the Father has loved me, so have I loved you. Now remain in my love. If you keep my commands, you will remain in my love, just as I have kept my Father's commands and remain in his love. I have told you this so that my joy may be in you and that your joy may be complete. My command is this: Love each other as I have loved you. Greater love has no one than this: to lay down one's life for one's friends. You are my friends if you do what I command. I no longer call you servants, because a servant does not know his master's business. Instead, I have called you friends, for everything that I learned from my Father I have made known to you. You did not choose me, but I chose you and appointed you so that you might go and bear fruit—fruit that will last—and so that whatever you ask in my name the Father will give you. This is my command: Love each other."

The day has begun. The flowers do sway in the morning breeze. Children are awakened to a prepared breakfast. The parents kiss each other quite affectionately in the love of the Lord.

The father gathers his family together and prays over each person, invoking the presence of the Lord to be on each person represented. The presence of the Lord falls on each one, leaving them with the glow of the Lord. At the same time, the Son Rises.

"The Call"

Ephesians 4:1-3

As a prisoner for the Lord, then, I urge you to live a life worthy of the calling you have received. Be completely humble and gentle; be patient, bearing with one another in love. Make every effort to keep the unity of the Spirit through the bond of peace.

Philippians 3:13-14

Brothers and sisters, I do not consider myself yet to have taken hold of it. But one thing I do: Forgetting what is behind and straining toward what is ahead, I press on toward the goal to win the prize for which God has called me heavenward in Christ Jesus.

God is calling His people to "get to work" in this hour. He has given us different gifts, which He desires to use for His glory. So, if you hear Him calling your name, listen, obey Him, and answer the call!!!

The call – answer it.

The call – walk it.

The call – live it.

The call – seize it.

The call – deliver it.

The call – proclaim it.

The call – see it.

The call – be it.

"The Goal"

Revelation 4

After this, I looked, and there before me was a door standing open in heaven. And the voice I had first heard speaking to me like a trumpet said, "Come up here, and I will show you what must take place after this." At once I was in the Spirit, and there before me was a throne in heaven with someone sitting on it. And the one who sat there had the appearance of jasper and ruby. A rainbow that shone like an emerald encircled the throne. Surrounding the throne were twenty-four other thrones, and seated on them were twenty-four elders. They were dressed in white and had crowns of gold on their heads. From the throne came flashes of lightning, rumblings and peals of thunder. In front of the throne, seven lamps were blazing. These are the seven spirits of God. Also in front of the throne, there was what looked like a sea of glass, clear as crystal. In the center, around the throne, were four living creatures, and they were covered with eyes, in front and in back. The first living creature was like a lion, the second was like an ox, the third had a face like a man, the fourth was like a flying eagle. Each of the four living creatures had six wings and was covered with eyes all around, even under its wings. Day and night, they never stop saying: "'Holy, holy, holy is the Lord God Almighty,' who was, and is, and is to come." Whenever the living creatures give glory, honor and thanks to him who sits on the throne and who lives forever and ever, the twenty-four elders fall down before him who sits on the throne and worship him who lives for ever and ever. They lay their crowns before the throne and say: "You are worthy, our Lord and God, to receive glory and honor and power, for you created all things, and by your will they were created and have their being."

We all must have a goal, and mine is standing before God and hearing Him say, "Child, well done. Enter into My rest." Heaven is my goal, and I want to live in God's rest with my Lord and Savior Jesus Christ for all eternity. Hope to see you there!

The goal is the object of every

Breath I take.

The goal is the object I fantasize

And dream about.

The goal is the place of my destination.

I cannot take my eyes off of it, nor

Can I turn my back to it.

The goal is real. The desire is pure.

All I can do is get to it.

About the Author

Rev. Dr. Gregory C. Wright, a native of Washington, DC, lives in the north Baltimore area. He is pastor of Fire Heart Ministries and is an online radio show host, "The Heart of Love Radio Show," among many other things. His purpose for writing this book is to encourage and bless people with inspirational poems, along with encouraging words, which are based from the Word of God.

From the Author

First, I would like to give glory to God for blessing and enabling me to put this book together 24 years ago. Next, I would like to thank my mom for encouraging me to release this book. Indeed, there is a time and a place for everything (Ecclesiastes 3), and I felt led to share this book with everyone right now. Also, I would like to thank my big sister Debra Johnson for helping me along this journey. Seeing her pursue her dreams inspired me to do the same. Finally, I would like to thank Illustrator George Franco for doing an excellent job! My prayer is that something written will touch your hearts and souls. God bless you!

©1997 Gregory Cecil Wright

www.ingramcontent.com/pod-product-compliance
Lightning Source LLC
Chambersburg PA
CBHW070042070426
42449CB00012BA/3142